JED PASCOE'S
THE FUNNY SIDE OF 30s

To Natalie

Welcome to the club!

Much love

Ali
x.

Published in the UK by
POWERFRESH Limited
21 Rothersthorpe Crescent
Northampton
NN4 8JD

Telephone   0845 130 4565
Facsimile   0845 130 4563

Copyright © 1993 Jed Pascoe

Cover and interior illustration

Cover and interior layout Powerfresh

ISBN 1902929128

All rights reserved. No part of this publication may be reproduced or transmitted in any form or by any means, electronic or mechanical, including photocopying, recording or any information storage and retrieval system, or for the source of ideas without the written permission of the publisher.

Printed in the UK by Belmont Press Northampton
Powerfresh First Imprint 1993 / New Edition 2000 reprint 2004

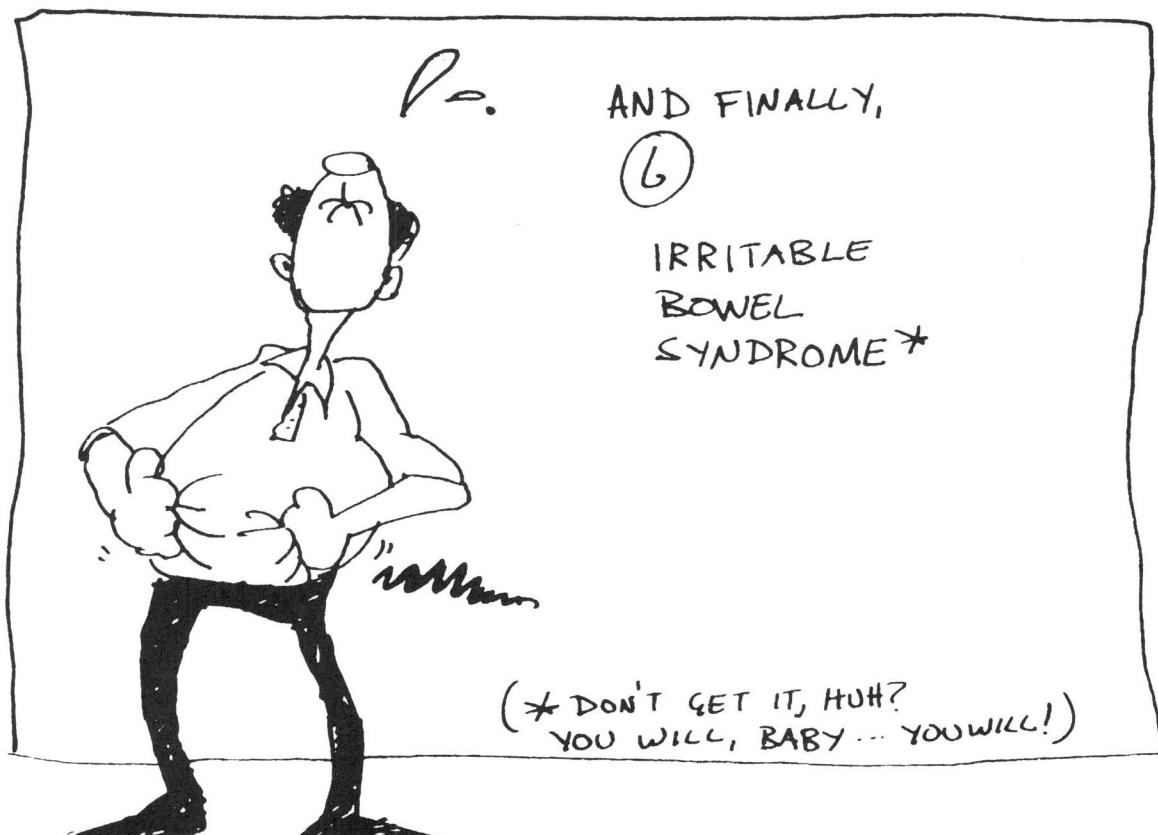

EMILY WOULD GO TO QUITE EXTRAORDINARY LENGTHS TO PREVENT A DOUBLE CHIN....

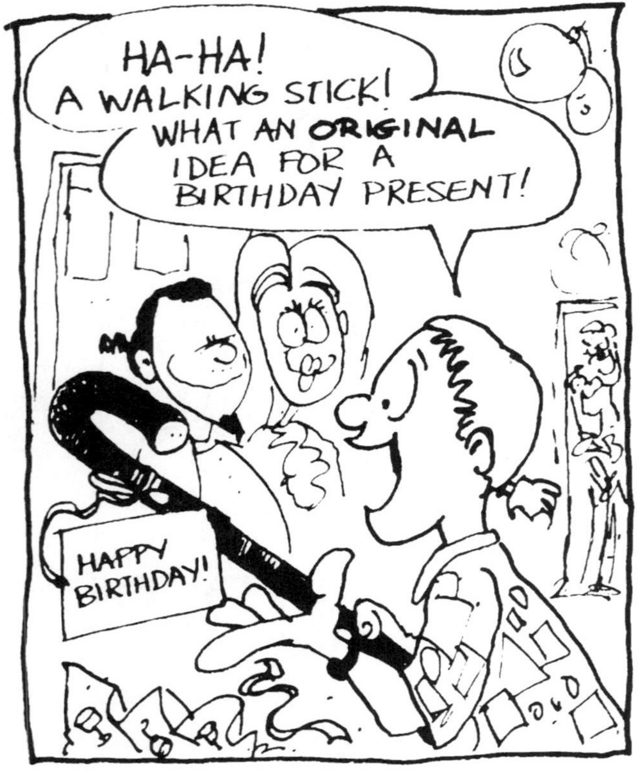

I'LL JUST PUT IT IN HERE UNTIL LATER...
GO AND JOIN THE OTHERS...
HAPPY BIRTHDAY

SIGH
HAPPY BIRTHDAY

KATHERINE HAD TO BE SURGICALLY REMOVED FROM HER SPORTS CAR IN FAVOUR OF A FAMILY ESTATE...

MY OBVIOUS WEALTH OF EXPERIENCE?
OK!

FRANKLY, IT WAS THE SHORTS...
!

RICHARD'S ATTEMPT TO KEEP ABREAST OF CONTEMPORARY HAIR STYLES FELL CATASTROPHICALLY SHORT OF THE MARK

I JUST THOUGHT IT WOULD MAKE A PLEASANT CHANGE IF WE SWAPPED DIETS
LAGER
XXX

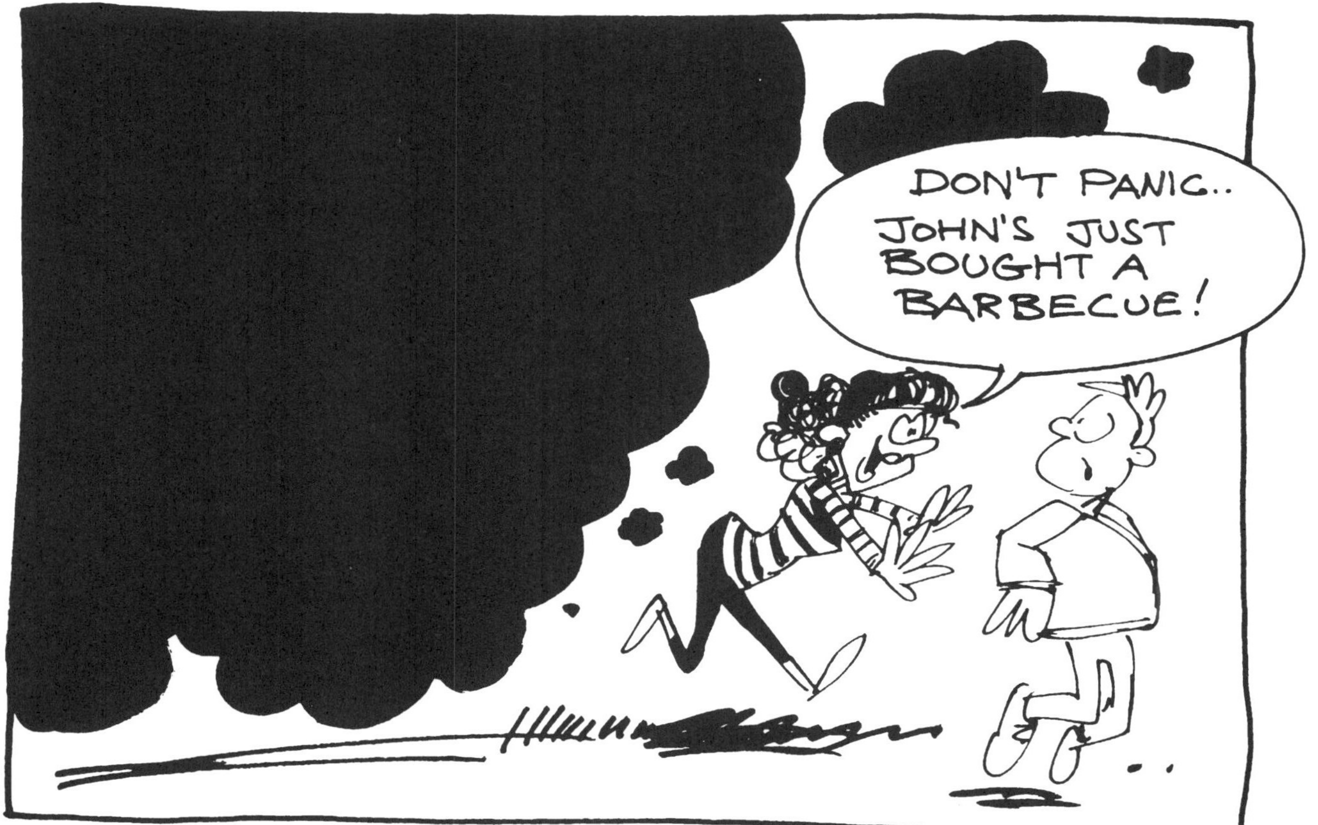
DON'T PANIC.. JOHN'S JUST BOUGHT A BARBECUE!

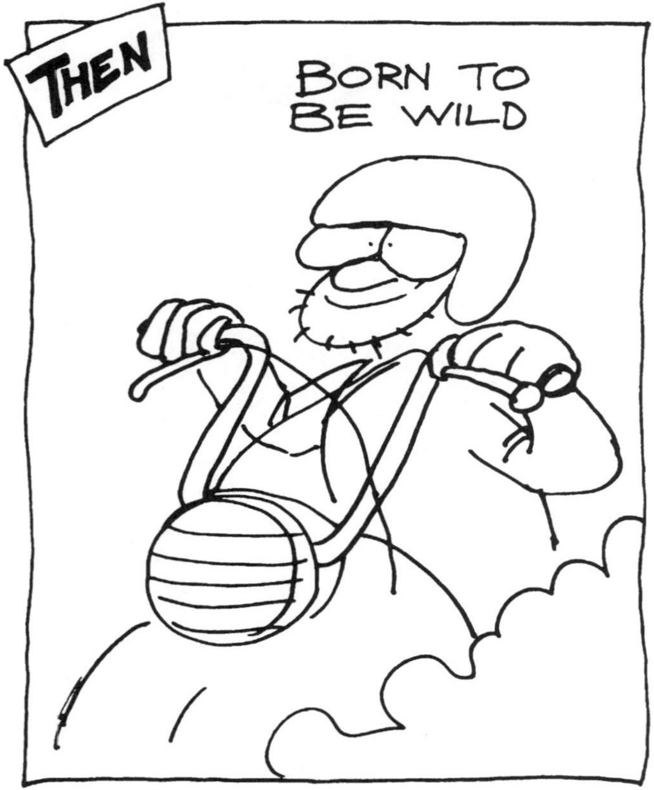
THEN
BORN TO
BE WILD

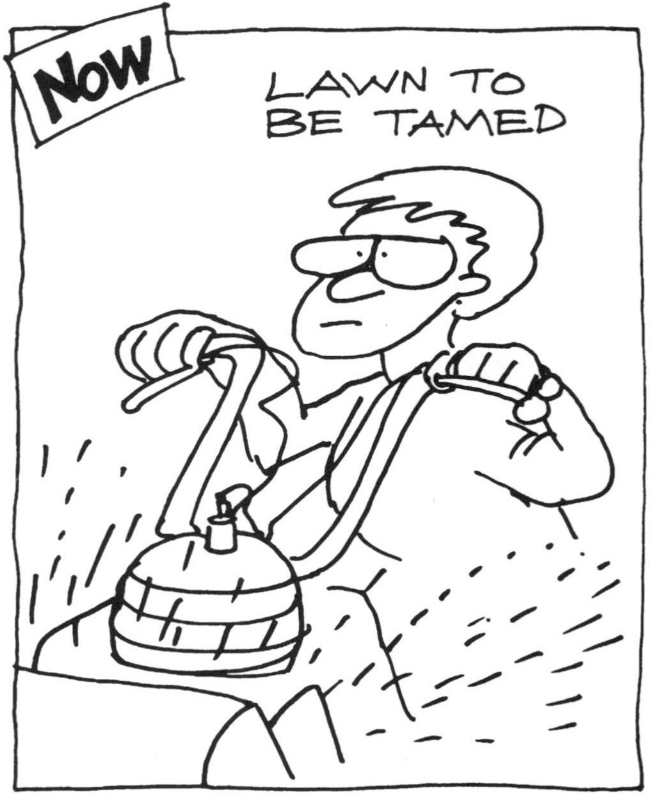
NOW
LAWN TO
BE TAMED

OVER-THE-HILL YUPPIE
PLEASE
BLESS YOU, GUV'NOR... SPARE A COPPER FOR A FINANCIAL TIMES...

GOLF?
HA! THAT'S AN OLD MAN'S SPORT!

NOW, RUGBY... THAT'S THE SPORT FOR FIT, YOUNG MEN LIKE ME!

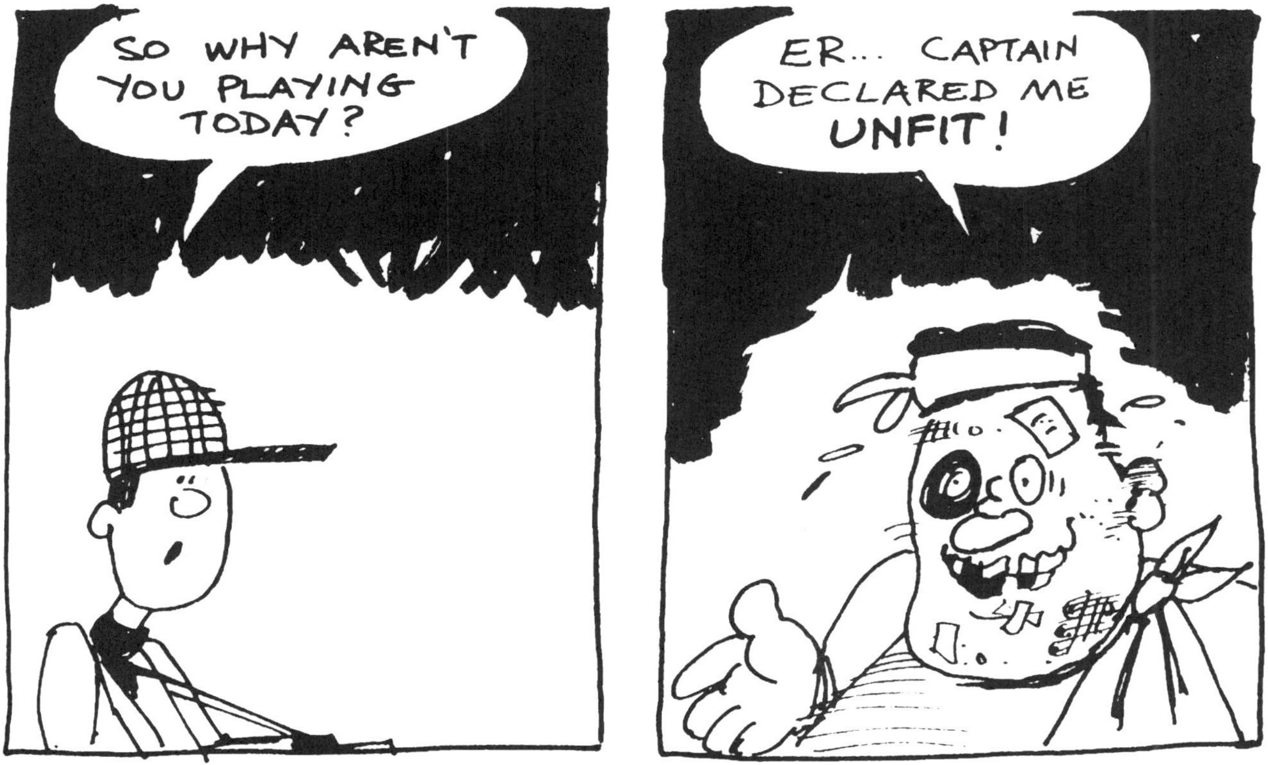
SO WHY AREN'T YOU PLAYING TODAY?
ER... CAPTAIN DECLARED ME UNFIT!

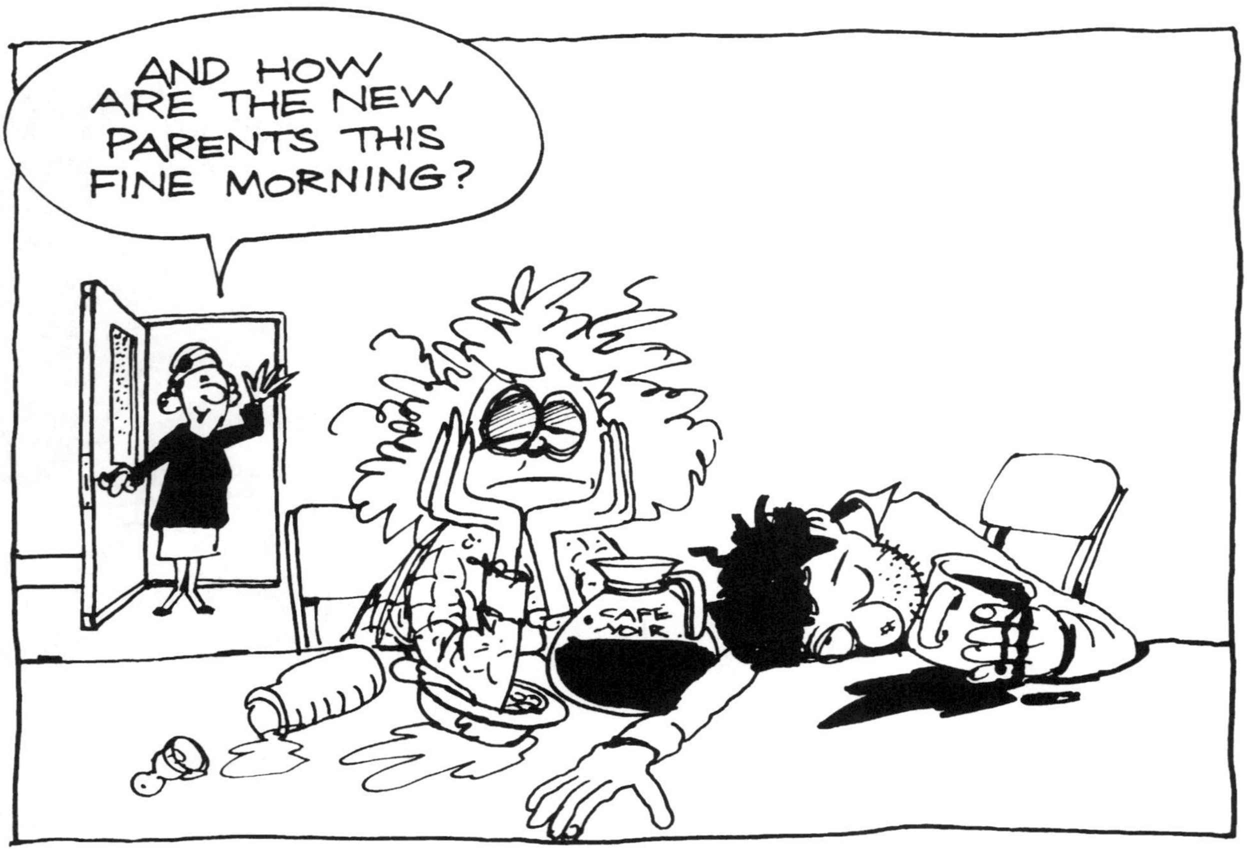
AND HOW ARE THE NEW PARENTS THIS FINE MORNING?
CAFÉ NOIR

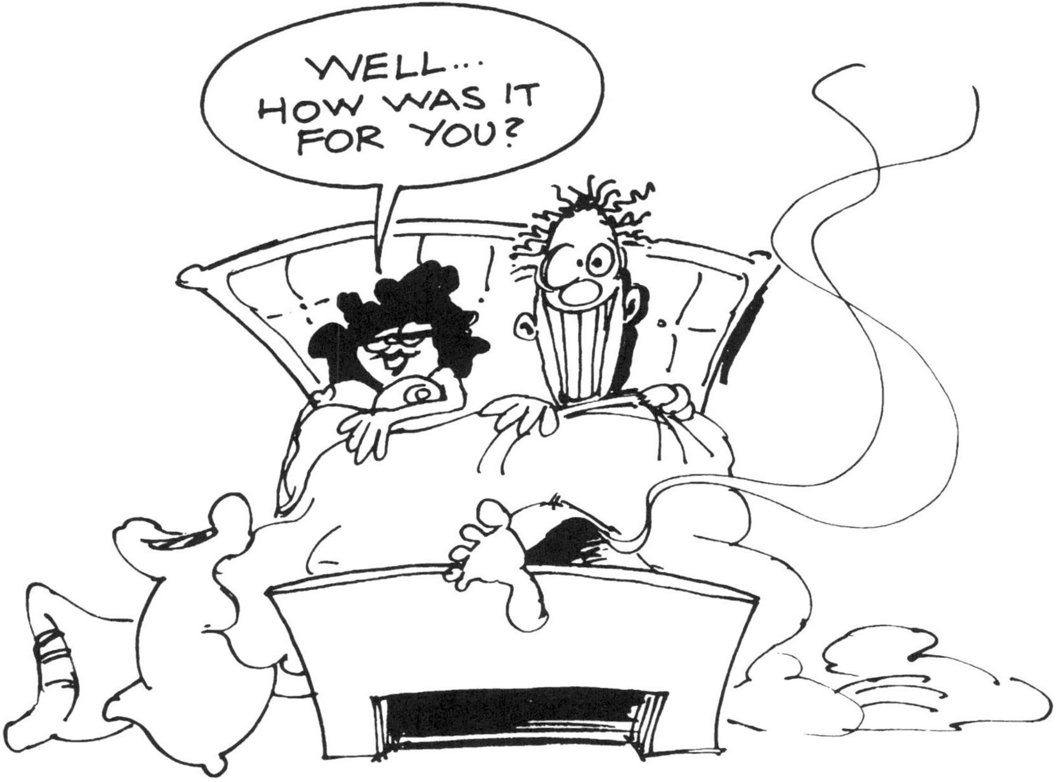
WELL...
HOW WAS IT
FOR YOU?

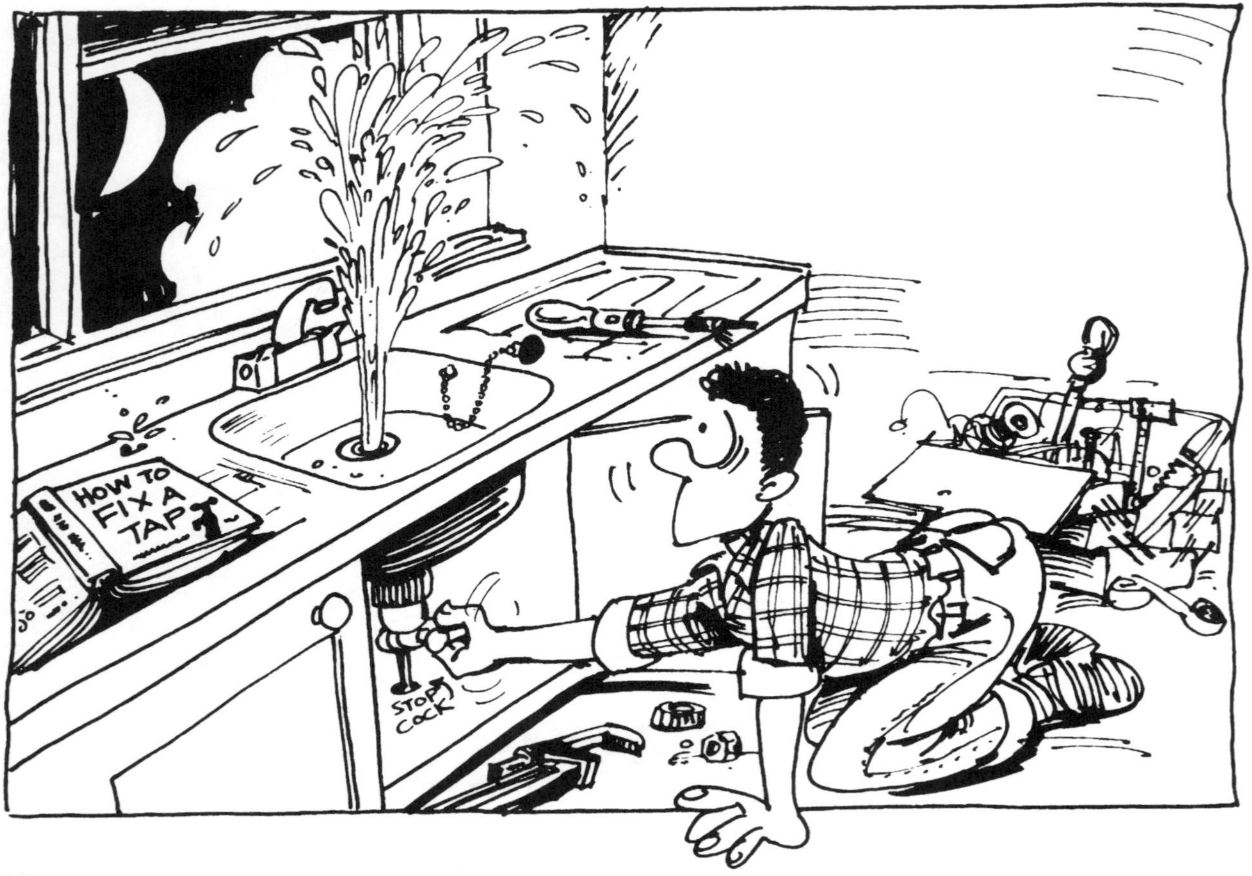
HOW TO FIX A TAP
STOP COCK

HI - DID I TELL YOU I'D REACHED THE FLIRTY THIRTIES?
YEAH - AND 'FLIRTY' IS ABOUT AS FAR AS YOU'LL GET THESE DAYS, OLD MAN...

1
MY MOTHER WAS RIGHT...
'A MOMENT ON THE LIPS,, A LIFETIME ON THE HIPS...'

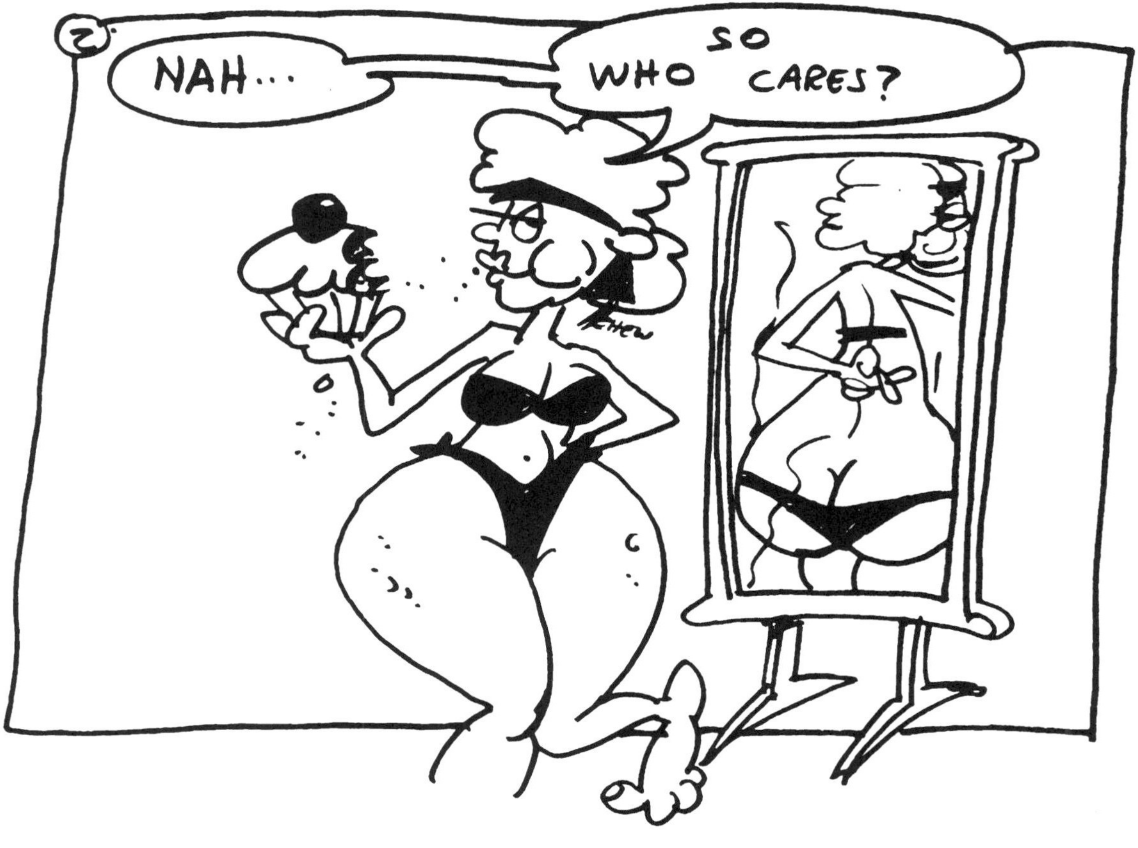
NAH...
SO WHO CARES?

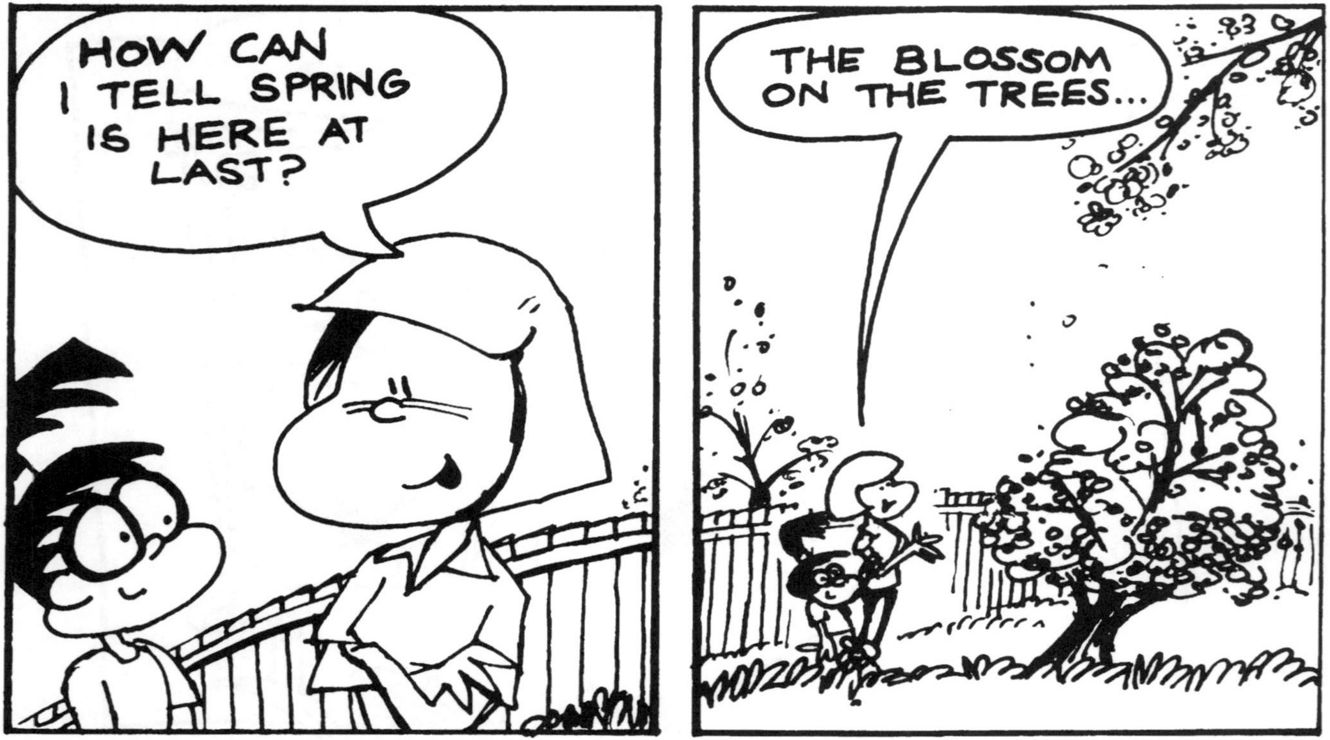
HOW CAN I TELL SPRING IS HERE AT LAST?
THE BLOSSOM ON THE TREES...

...THE BIRDS BUILDING NESTS...
...AND YOUR FATHER TRYING OUT HIS FLY-FISHING TACKLE..
JED PASCOE

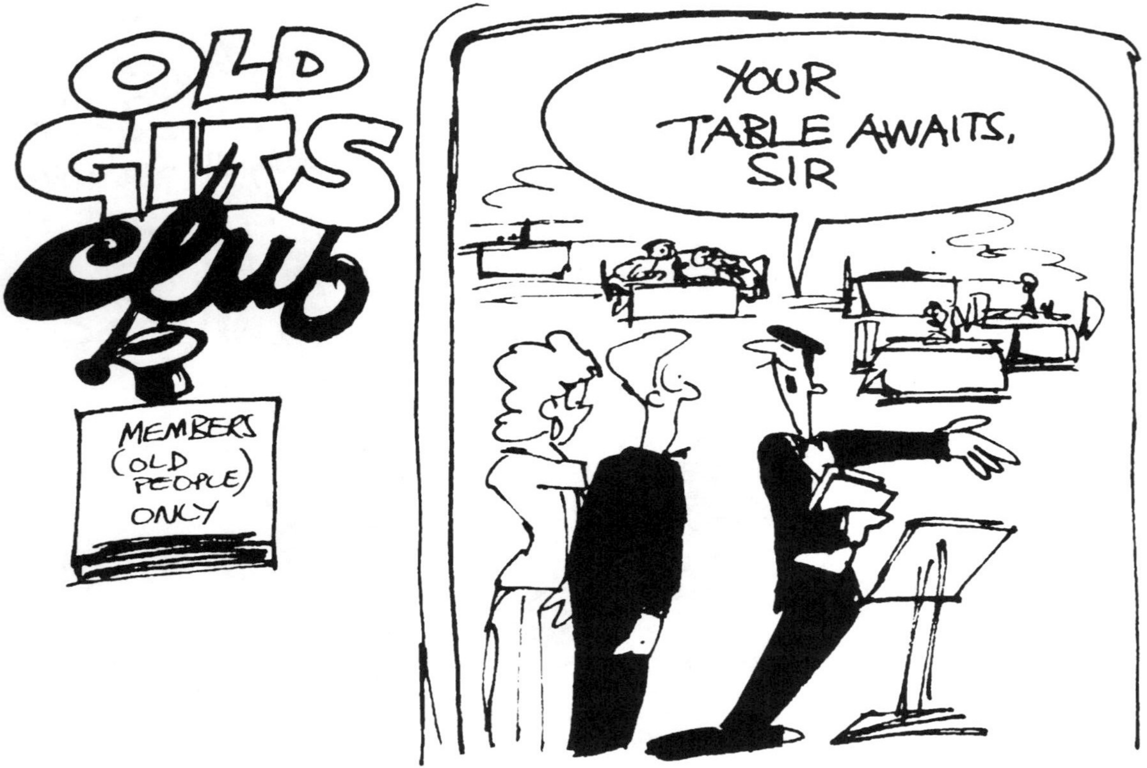
OLD GITS Club
MEMBERS (OLD PEOPLE) ONLY
YOUR TABLE AWAITS, SIR

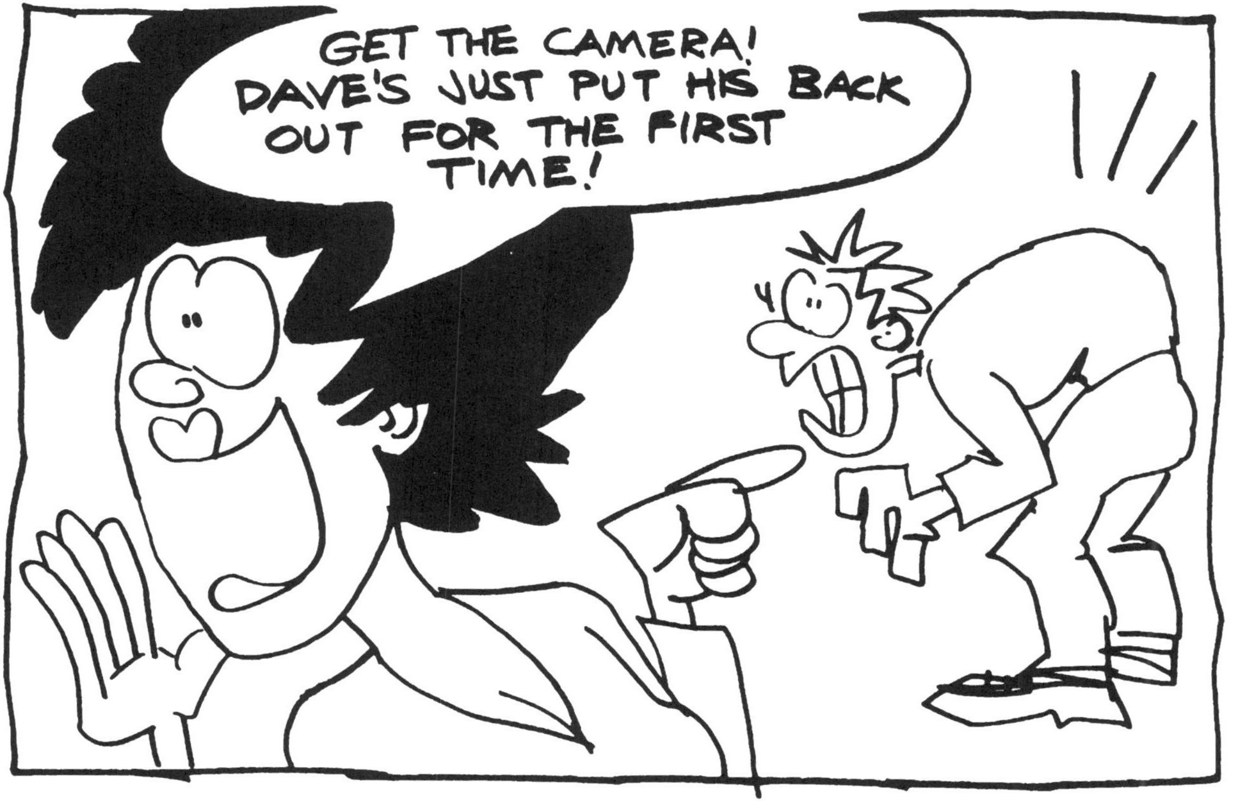
GET THE CAMERA! DAVE'S JUST PUT HIS BACK OUT FOR THE FIRST TIME!

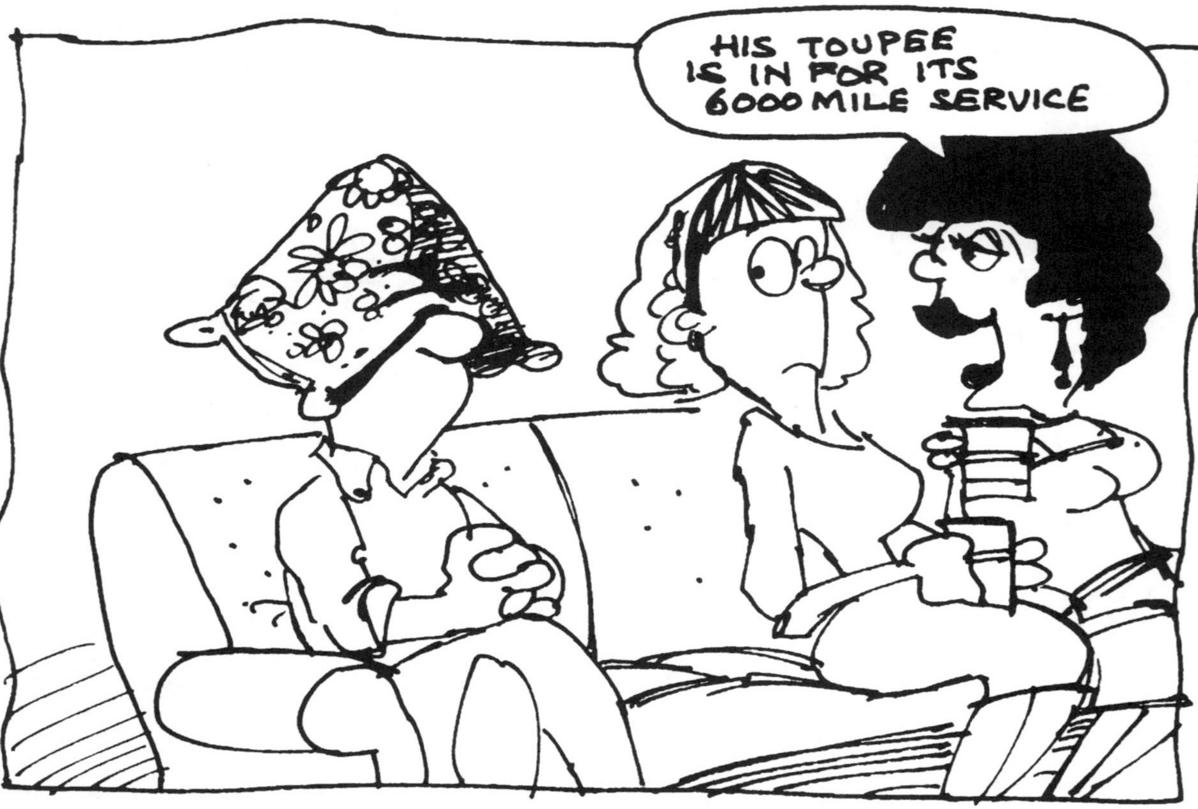
HIS TOUPEE IS IN FOR ITS 6000 MILE SERVICE

WARBLE
I AM SIXTEEN, ♫ GOING ON SEVENTEEN ♫
THE SOUND OF MUSIC
I AM 30, GOING ON A TREADMILL

SCREEN 1
SCREEN 2
ONE OF THE ADVANTAGES OF HAVING A YOUNG FAMILY IS WE CAN ENJOY A DISNEY WITHOUT FEELING EMBARRASSED....!

I'M THE ONLY SANTA IN THE STREET TO BE SUSSED BY THE UNDER-FIVES...

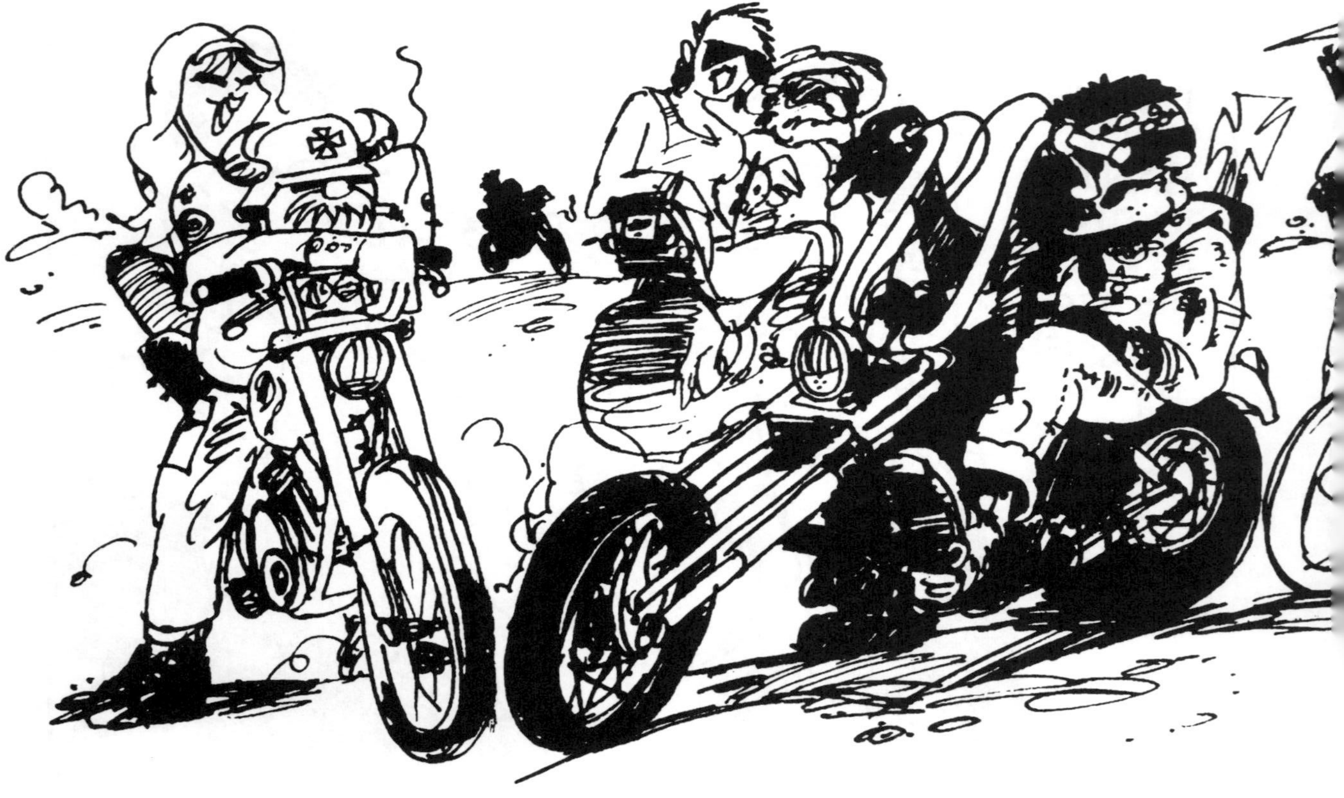

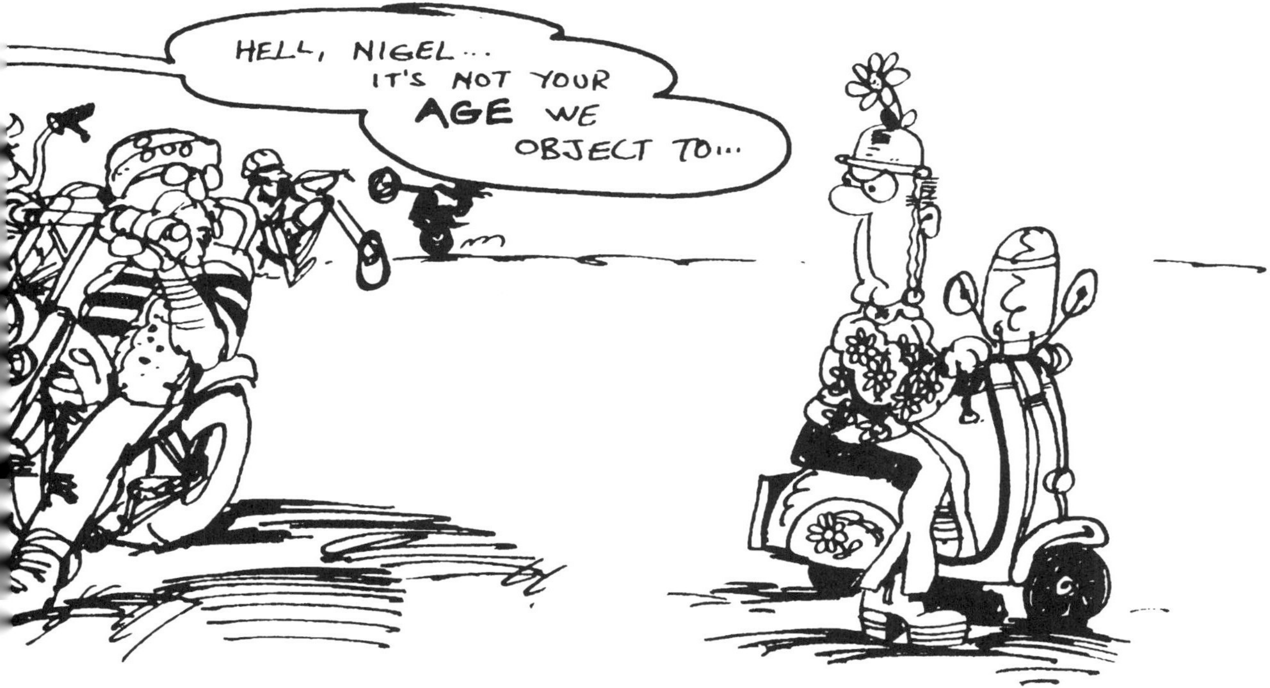
HELL, NIGEL...
IT'S NOT YOUR
AGE WE
OBJECT TO...

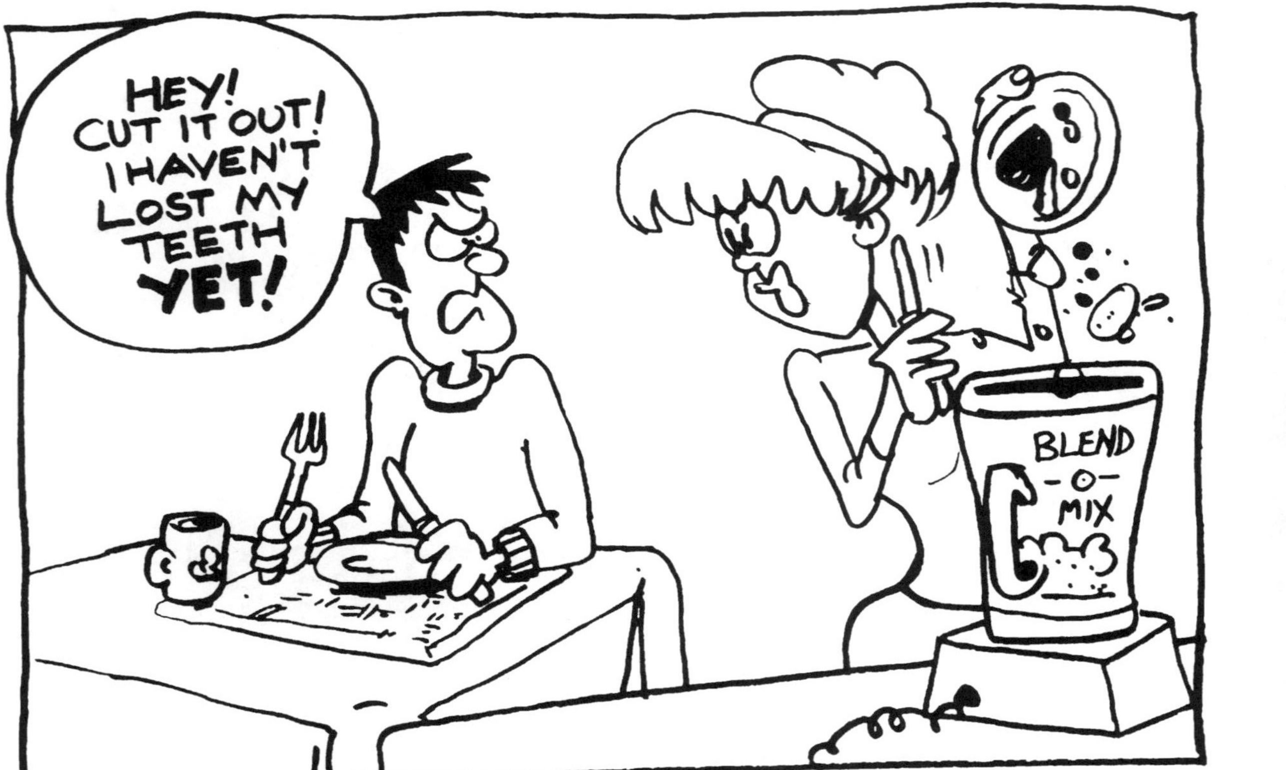
HEY! CUT IT OUT! I HAVEN'T LOST MY TEETH YET!
BLEND -O- MIX

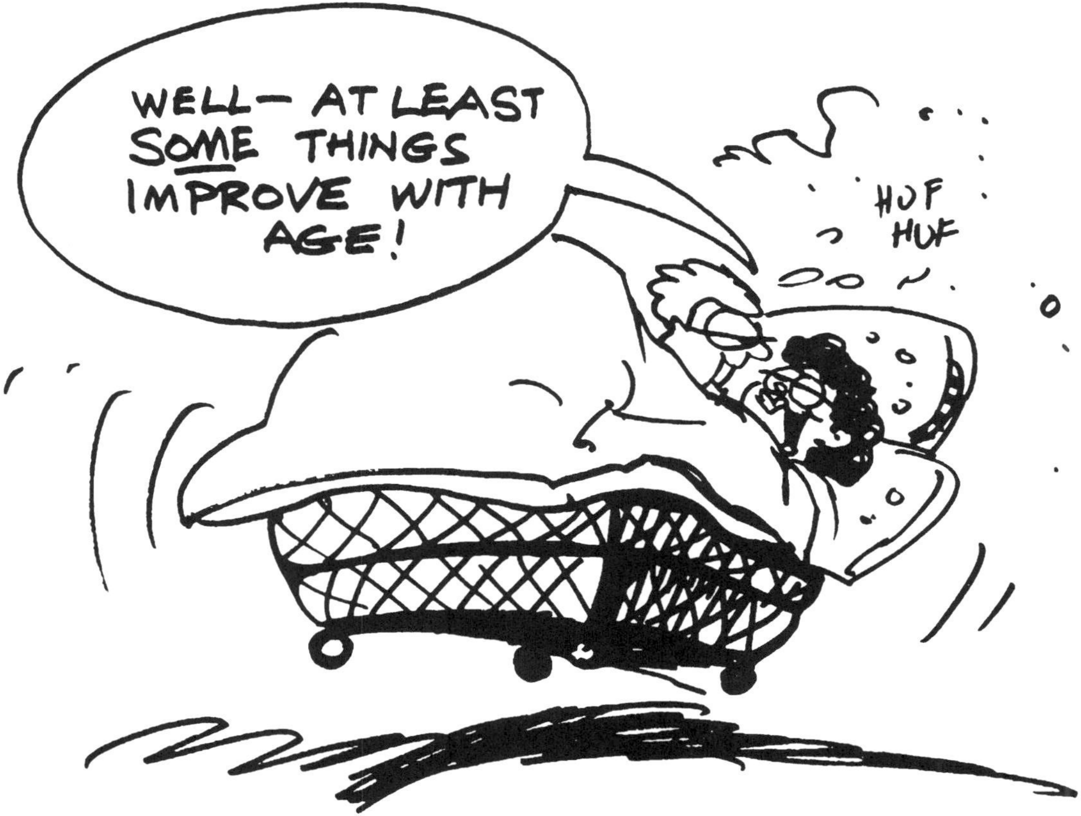
WELL— AT LEAST SOME THINGS IMPROVE WITH AGE!
HUF HUF

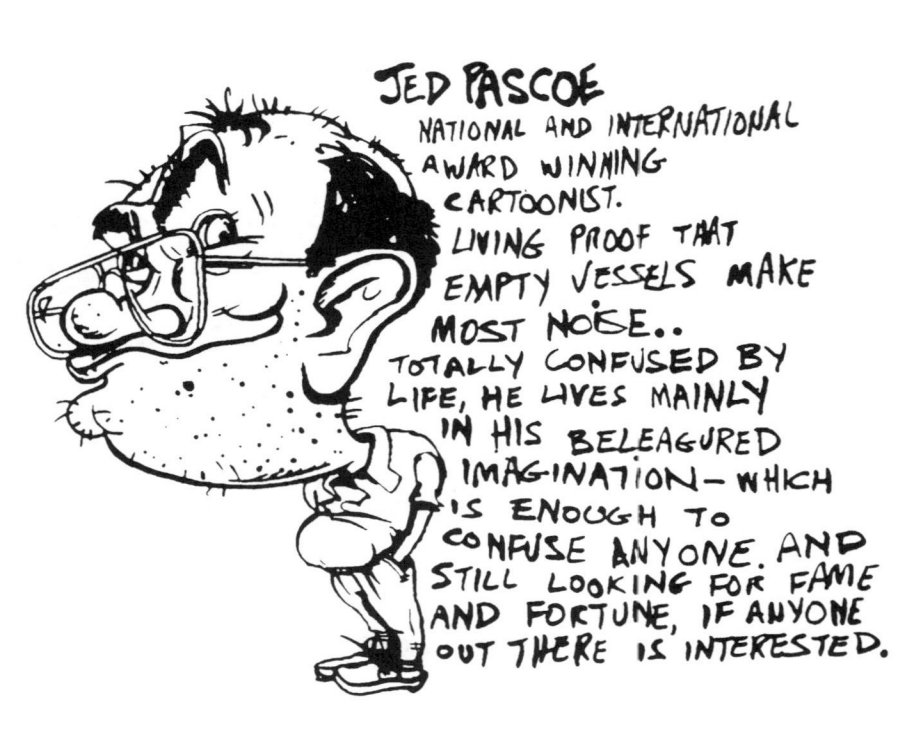

JED PASCOE
NATIONAL AND INTERNATIONAL AWARD WINNING CARTOONIST. LIVING PROOF THAT EMPTY VESSELS MAKE MOST NOISE.. TOTALLY CONFUSED BY LIFE, HE LIVES MAINLY IN HIS BELEAGURED IMAGINATION — WHICH IS ENOUGH TO CONFUSE ANYONE. AND STILL LOOKING FOR FAME AND FORTUNE, IF ANYONE OUT THERE IS INTERESTED.

other POWERFRESH titles

POWERFRESH TONI GOFFE TITLES
1902929411	FINISHED AT 50	2.99	☐
1902929403	FARTING	2.99	☐
190292942X	LIFE AFTER BABY	2.99	☐

POWERFRESH MAD SERIES
1874125783	MAD TO BE FATHER	2.99	☐
1874125694	MAD TO BE A MOTHER	2.99	☐
1874125686	MAD ON FOOTBALL	2.99	☐
187412552X	MAD TO GET MARRIED	2.99	☐
1874125546	MAD TO HAVE A BABY	2.99	☐
1874125619	MAD TO HAVE A PONY	2.99	☐
1874125627	MAD TO HAVE A CAT	2.99	☐
1874125643	MAD TO BE 40 HIM	2.99	☐
1874125651	MAD TO BE 40 HER	2.99	☐
187412566X	MAD TO BE 50 HIM	2.99	☐

POWERFRESH FUNNYSIDE SERIES
1874125260	FUNNY SIDE OF 30	2.99	☐
1874125104	FUNNY SIDE OF 40 HIM	2.99	☐
1874125112	FUNNY SIDE OF 40 HER	2.99	☐
190292911X	FUNNY SIDE OF 50 HIM	2.99	☐
1874125139	FUNNY SIDE OF 50 HER	2.99	☐
1874125252	FUNNY SIDE OF 60	2.99	☐
1874125279	FUNNY SIDE OF SEX	2.99	☐

POWERFRESH OTHER A5
1874125171	"CRINKLED ""N"" WRINKLED"	2.99	☐
1874125376	A MOTHER NO FUN	2.99	☐
1874125449	WE'REGETTING MARRIED	2.99	☐
1874125481	CATCRAZY	2.99	☐
190292908X	EVERYTHING MEN KNOW ABOUT SEX	2.99	☐
1902929071	EVERYTHING MEN KNOW ABOUT WMN	2.99	☐
1902929004	KISSING COURSE	2.99	☐
1874125996	CONGRATULATIONS YOU'VE PASSED	2.99	☐
1902929276	TOILET VISITORS BOOK	2.99	☐
1902929160	BIG FAT SLEEPY CAT	2.99	☐

POWERFRESH SILVEY JEX TITLES
1902929055	FART ATTACK	2.99	☐
1874125961	LOVE & PASSION 4 THE ELEDRLY	2.99	☐
187412597X	A BABY BOOK	2.99	☐
1874125996	SHEEP 'N' NASTY	2.99	☐
1874125988	SPORT FOR THE ELDERLY	2.99	☐
1902929144	FUN & FROLICS FOR THE ELDERLY	2.99	☐

POWERFRESH HUMOUR
1874125945	GUIDE TO SEX & SEDUCTION	3.99	☐
1874125848	DICK'S NAUGHTY BOOK	3.99	☐
190292925X	MODERN BABES LB OF SPELLS	4.99	☐
1902929268	A MUMS LB OF SPELLS	4.99	☐

POWERFRESH LITTLE SQUARE TITLES
1902929330	LS DIRTY JOKES	2.50	☐
1902929314	LS DRINKING JOKES	2.50	☐
1902929322	LS GOLF JOKES	2.50	☐
190292939X	LS IRISH JOKES	2.50	☐
1902929292	LS TURNING 18	2.50	☐
1902929241	LS THE BIG 40	2.50	☐
1902929233	LS THE BIG 50	2.50	☐
1902929284	LS BIG 60	2.50	☐
1902929225	LS SINGLE V MARRIED WOMEN	2.50	☐
1902929217	LS YES BUT...!	2.50	☐
1902929306	LS WHISKY	2.50	☐
1902929500	LS HOW TO PULL BY MAGIC	2.50	☐

POWERFRESH STATIONARY TITLES
1902929381	WEDDING GUEST BOOK	9.99	☐
1902929349	WEEKLY PLANNER CATS	6.99	☐
1902929357	WEEKLY PLANNER DOGS	6.99	☐
1902929365	WEEKLY PLANNER COTTAGES	6.99	☐
1902929373	WEEKLY PLANNER OFFICE	6.99	☐
1902929519	HUMDINGER TELEPHONE BOOK	4.99	☐
1902929527	HUMDINGER ADDRESS BOOK	4.99	☐
1902929535	HUMDINGER NOTEBOOK	2.99	☐

Name

Address

P&P £1.00 Per Parcel

Please send cheques payable to Powerfresh LTD

To Powerfresh LTD 21 Rothersthorpe Crescent Northampton NN4 8JD